Book One

Listening and Speaking Activities for Beginning Students of English

John R. Boyd · Mary Ann Boyd

PRENTICE HALL REGENTS
A VIACOM COMPANY
Upper Saddle River, NJ 07458

02379

Publisher: Mary Jane Peluso

Development Editor: Carol Callahan

Electronic Composition: Alan Haimowitz

Electronic Production Editor: Carey Davies

Manufacturing Manager: Ray Keating

Cover Art: Bruce Kenselaar

Cover Design: Bruce Kenselaar

Art Director: Merle Krumper

Electronic Art / Realia: North Market Street Graphics

Electronic Art Production Supervisor: Todd Ware

Electronic Art Production Specialist: Marita Froimson

PRENTICE HALL REGENTS
A VIACOM COMPANY

© 1996 by Prentice Hall Regents
Prentice-Hall, Inc.
A Simon & Schuster Company
Upper Saddle River, NJ 07458

Printed in the United States of America

10 9 8 7 6 5 4 3 2 1

ISBN 0-13-299785-1

Prentice Hall International (UK) Limited, London
Prentice Hall of Australia Pty. Limited, Sydney
Prentice Hall Canada, Inc., Toronto
Prentice Hall Hispanoamericana, S.A., Mexico
Prentice Hall of India Private Limited, New Delhi
Prentice Hall of Japan, Inc., Tokyo
Simon & Schuster Asia Pte. Ltd., Singapore
Editora Prentice Hall do Brasil, Ltda., Rio de Janeiro

INTRODUCTORY UNIT
REVIEW OF NUMBERS AND LETTERS

1	2	3	4	5

PRACTICE A

	A	B	C
1.	1:05	1:02	1:03
2.	2:04	2:01	2:05
3.	3:02	3:03	3:05
4.	4:05	4:01	4:02
5.	5:04	5:05	5:01
6.	1:05	1:02	1:04
7.	2:04	2:05	2:02
8.	3:05	3:04	3:01
9.	4:01	4:03	4:05
10.	5:02	5:05	5:03

1	2	3	4	5	6	7	8	9

PRACTICE B

	A	B	C
1.	212–3213	212–3123	212–3132
2.	323–4312	323–4132	323–4321
3.	434–5341	434–5431	434–5314
4.	545–6432	545–6324	545–6342
5.	656–7543	656–7453	656–7534
6.	555–767–8654	555–767–8645	555–767–8564
7.	555–878–9765	555–878–9756	555–878–9675
8.	555–989–0876	555–989–0867	555–989–0786
9.	555–807–9231	555–807–9213	555–807–9321
10.	555–605–4056	555–605–4065	555–605–4005

PRACTICE C

1. A B C D (E) F G H I (J) K L M N O P Q R S T U V W X Y Z

2. a b c d e f g h i j k l m n o p q r s t u v w x y z

3. A B C D E F G H I J K L M N O P Q R S T U V W X Y Z

4. A B C D E F G H I J K L M N O P Q R S T U V W X Y Z

5. a b c d e f g h i j k l m n o p q r s t u v w x y z

6. A B C D E F G H I J K L M N O P Q R S T U V W X Y Z

7. A B C D E F G H I J K L M N O P Q R S T U V W X Y Z

8. A B C D E F G H I J K L M N O P Q R S T U V W X Y Z

9. a b c d e f g h i j k l m n o p q r s t u v w x y z

10. A B C D E F G H I J K L M N O P Q R S T U V W X Y Z

PRACTICE D

A B C D E F G H I J K L M N O P Q R S T U V W X Y Z

a b c d e f g h i j k l m n o p q r s t u v w x y z

| 1 | 2 | 3 | 4 | 5 | 6 | 7 | 8 | 9 | 10 | 11 | 12 | 13 | 14 | 15 | 16 | 17 | 18 | 19 | 20 |

PRACTICE E

	A	**B**	**C**
1.	$17.10	$17.20	$17.05
2.	$13.04	$13.14	$13.05
3.	$14.08	$14.01	$14.18
4.	$19.11	$19.05	$19.20
5.	$10.04	$10.07	$10.10
6.	$18.01	$18.05	$18.15
7.	$12.02	$12.20	$12.10
8.	$15.05	$15.10	$15.20
9.	$16.08	$16.18	$16.10
10.	$11.19	$11.03	$11.07

PRACTICE F

1

_o n e_

2

— — —

3

— — — — —

4

— — — —

5

— — — —

6

— — —

7

— — — — — —

8

— — — — — —

9

— — — —

10

— — —

11

— — — — — —

12

— — — — — —

13

— — — — — — —

14

— — — — — — —

15

— — — — — —

16

— — — — — — —

17

— — — — — — — —

18

— — — — — — —

19

— — — — — —

20

— — — — —

UNIT 1   COLORS

PRESENTATION A

PRACTICE A

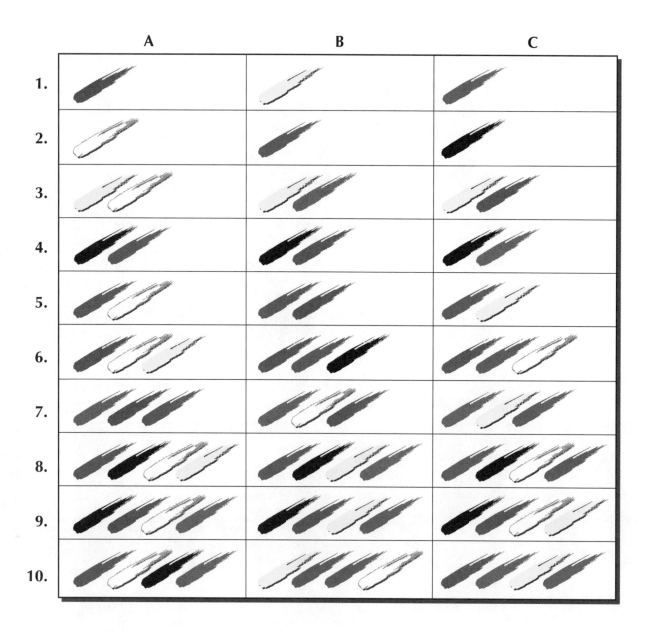

PRESENTATION B

1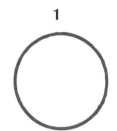

2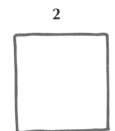

3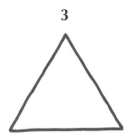

PRACTICE B

	A	B	C
1.	⬤	⬤	◯
2.	☐	▢	▢
3.	▲	△	▲
4.	⬤	▢	▲
5.	▲	⬤	▪
6.	⬤ ☐	⬤ ▢	⬤ ☐
7.	▲ ◯	▲ ◯	▲ ⬤
8.	☐ △ ⬤	☐ △ ⬤	☐ △ ⬤
9.	⬤ ▢ ◺	⬤ ▲ ☐	⬤ ⬤ △
10.	▲ ◯ ☐ ▪	▲ ☐ ◯ ⬤	▲ ◯ ◯ ▪

7

PRESENTATION C

PRACTICE C

Part 1

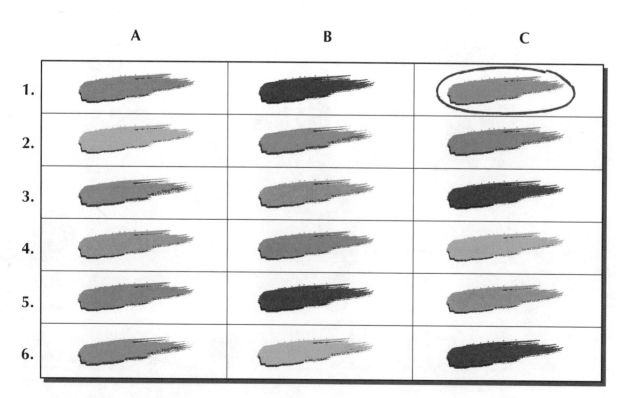

Part 2

	A	B	C
1.			
2.			
3.			
4.			
5.			
6.			

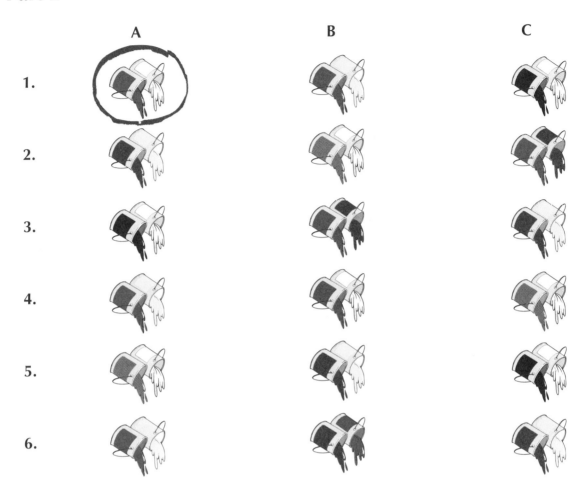

PRACTICE D

Part 1

1. _____14_____   5. _____   9. _____

2. _____   6. _____   10. _____

3. _____   7. _____   11. _____

4. _____   8. _____   12. _____

Part 2

	A	B	C
1.			
2.			
3.			
4.			
5.			
6.			
7.			
8.			
9.			
10.			

PRACTICE E

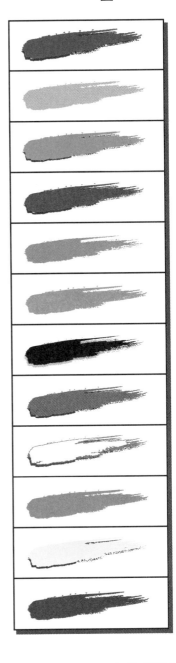

1. <u>r</u> <u>e</u> <u>d</u>

2. ___ ___ ___

3. ___ ___ ___

4. ___ ___ ___ ___

5. ___ ___ ___ ___

6. ___ ___ ___ ___ ___

7. ___ ___ ___ ___ ___

8. ___ ___ ___ ___ ___

9. ___ ___ ___ ___

10. ___ ___ ___ ___ ___

11. ___ ___ ___ ___ ___

12. ___ ___ ___ ___ ___ ___

READ & WRITE

1. Red and <u>w</u> <u>h</u> <u>i</u> <u>t</u> <u>e</u> make pink.

2. Black and white make ___ ___ ___ ___ .

3. Red and ___ ___ ___ ___ ___ ___ make orange.

4. Blue and yellow make ___ ___ ___ ___ ___ .

5. ___ ___ ___ ___ ___ and white make ___ ___ ___ .

6. Red and ___ ___ ___ ___ make ___ ___ ___ ___ ___ ___ .

UNIT REVIEW

Part 1

1

2

3

4

Part 2

	1.	2.	3.	4.	5.	6.	7.	8.	9.	10.	11.	12.
Yes	✓											
No												

The square is red.

The squares are red.

The girl is wearing red.

The girls are wearing red.

Part 3

1. The boy in the red car _____ wearing blue.

2. The girls in the yellow car _____ wearing pink.

3. The boy and the girl in the green car _____ wearing brown and tan.

4. 111 _____ the red car.

5. 12 and 15 _____ the yellow and green cars.

Part 4

The three cars ∧red, yellow, and green. On the doors of the cars squares, triangles, and circles. The red car 111. The number 111 in the circle between the triangles. The yellow car 12. The number 12 in the triangle between the squares. Where the number 55?

I am wearing red.

You are wearing red.

He is wearing red.

She is wearing red.

We are wearing red.

You are wearing red.

They are wearing red.

UNIT 2 *NATIONALITIES*

PRESENTATION A

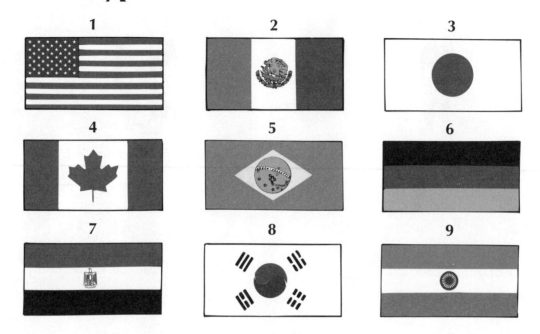

PRACTICE A

Part 1

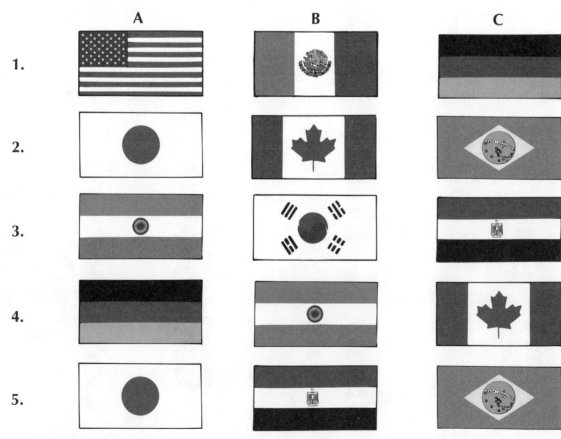

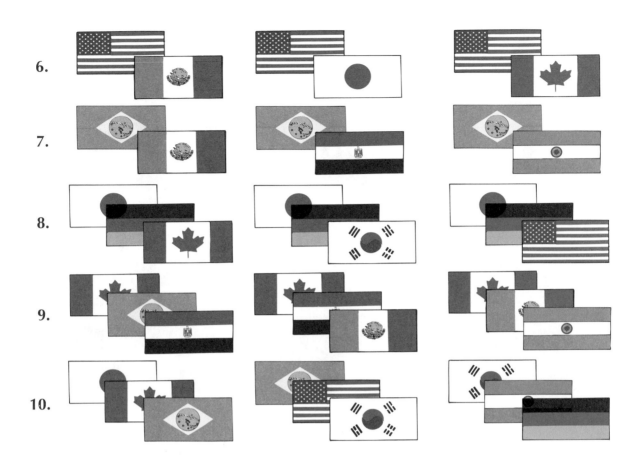

Part 2

	1.	2.	3.	4.	5.	6.	7.	8.	9.	10.
Yes										
No										

PRESENTATION B

	A	B	C
1.			
2.			
3.			
4.			
5.			
6.			
7.			
8.			

READ & WRITE

Part 1

A Canadian in a Japanese car. He has Canadian flags. An American in a German car, and she wearing red, and blue. A Japanese in a Korean car. He has Japanese flags. Who in the American car, and what she wearing?

Part 2

1. __ __ __ __ __ __

2. __ __ __ __ __ __

3. __ __ __ __ __ __

4. __ __ __ __ __ __ __

5. __ __ __ __ __ __ __ __

6. __ __ __ __ __ __ __ __ __

7. __ __ __ __ __ __ __

8. __ __ __ __ __ __ __

9. __ __ __ __ __ __ __

Part 3

1. The _____ flag is black, red, and yellow.

2. The _____ flag is orange, white and green.

3. The _____ flag is green, yellow, and blue.

4. The _____ flag is green, white, and red.

5. The _____ flag is red, white, and blue.

6. The _____ flag is red, white, and black.

7. The _____ flag is red, blue, white, and black.

8. The _____ flag and the _____ flag are red and white.

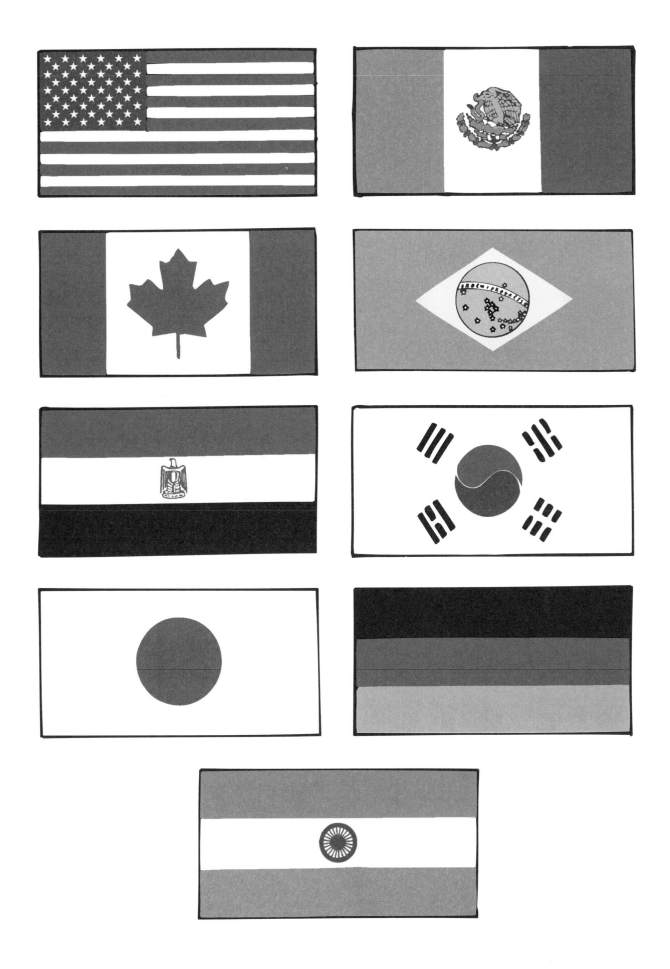

UNIT 3   COUNTRIES

PRESENTATION A

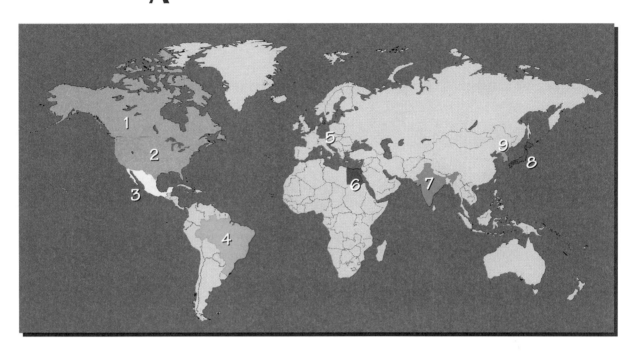

PRACTICE A

Part 1

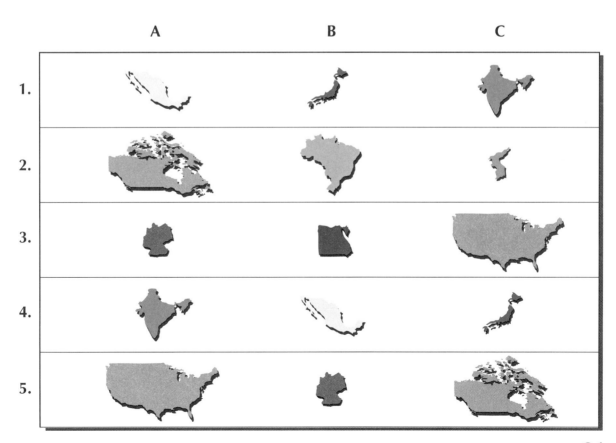

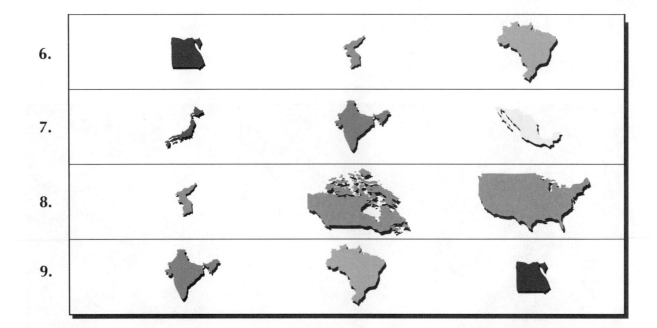

Part 2

1. __ __ __ __ __

2. __ __ __ __ __

3. __ __ __ __ __

4. __ __ __ __ __

5. __ __ __ __ __ __ __

6. __ __ __ __ __

7. __ __ __ __ __ __

8. __ __ __ __ __ __

9. the __ __ __ __ __ __ __ __ __ __ __

PRESENTATION B

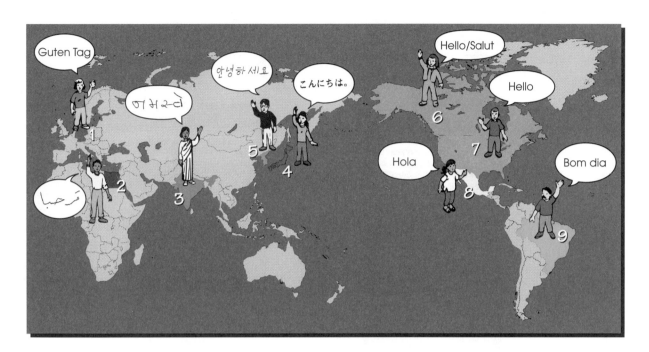

PRACTICE B

Part 1

	1.	2.	3.	4.	5.	6.	7.	8.	9.	10.
Yes										
No										

Part 2

1.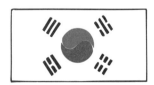

2.

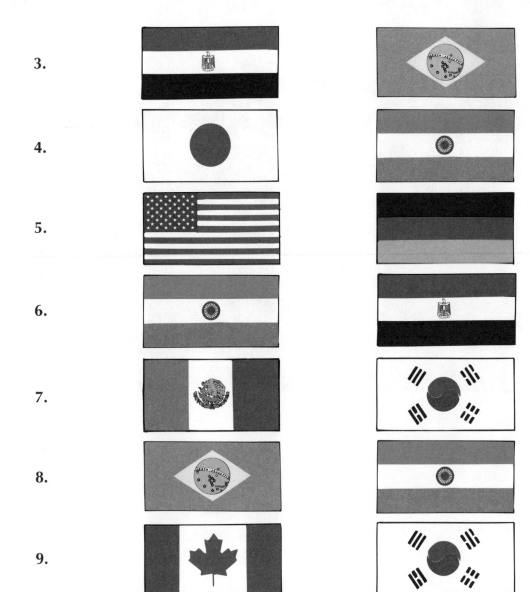

3.

4.

5.

6.

7.

8.

9.

READ & WRITE

Part 1

1. __ __ __ __ __ __ __

2. __ __ __ __ __ __

3. __ __ __ __ __ __ __ __

4. __ __ __ __ __ __

5. __ __ __ __ __

6. __ __ __ __ __ __

7. __ __ __ __ __ __ __

8. __ __ __ __ __ __

9. __ __ __ __ __ __ __ __ __

Part 2

1. They speak _____ in Japan.
2. They speak _____ in Mexico.
3. They speak _____ in Germany.
4. They speak _____ in Korea.
5. They speak _____ and _____ in India.
6. They speak _____ in Egypt.
7. They speak _____ in Brazil.
8. They speak _____ and _____ in Canada.
9. They speak _____ in the United States.

Part 3

In Korea they Korean. In Japan speak Japanese. Mexico do they speak Mexican? No, speak Spanish. In Brazil do they Brazilian? No, they speak Portuguese. The Germans speak but the Egyptians don't Egyptian. They speak Arabic. The French speak but the Indians don't Indian. They speak Hindi.

He <u>speaks</u>.   She <u>speaks</u>.   They <u>speak</u>.   He and she <u>speak</u>.

Part 4

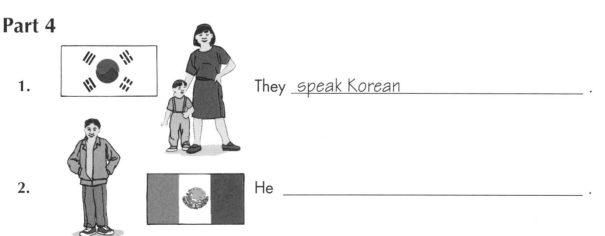

1. They _speak Korean_____ .

2. He _____ .

25

3. She _____ .

4. They _____ and

_____ .

5. He _____ .

6. She _____ .

7. He _____ .

8. They _____ and

_____ .

9. He and she _____ .

A	B	C	D	E	F	G	H	I	J
10	20	30	40	50	60	70	80	90	100

PRACTICE C

Part 1

	1.	2.	3.	4.	5.	6.	7.	8.	9.	10.
Yes										
No										

Part 2

1.	$22.50	$22.60	$22.80
2.	$34.70	$34.10	$34.90
3.	$43.20	$43.22	$43.12
4.	$55.90	$55.19	$55.99
5.	$67.17	$67.11	$67.49
6.	$78.13	$78.33	$78.39
7.	$89.15	$89.12	$89.14
8.	$91.90	$91.19	$91.99
9.	$114.50	$114.15	$111.40
10.	$312.49	$311.49	$314.49

PRESENTATION D

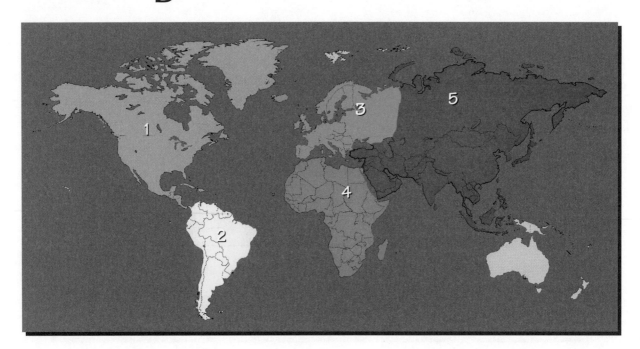

PRACTICE D

Part 1

1. __ __ __ __

2. __ __ __ __ __ __

3. __ __ __ __ __

4. __ __ __ __ __ __ __ __ __ __ __

5. __ __ __ __ __ __ __ __ __ __ __

Part 2

1. North America   South America

2. Asia   Europe

3. Europe   North America

4. North America   Asia

5. Africa   South America

6. North America   Africa

7. Africa   Asia

8. Europe   Asia

9. Asia   Africa

READ & WRITE

Part 1

In America they speak European languages. In Mexico they Spanish, in the United States they speak, and in Canada speak and French. In America they speak except in Brazil where they Portuguese.

Part 2

1. Germany is in _____.

2. Egypt is in _____.

3. Brazil is in _____.

4. India is in _____.

5. Japan is in _____.

6. Canada, the United States, and Mexico are in _____.

PRESENTATION E

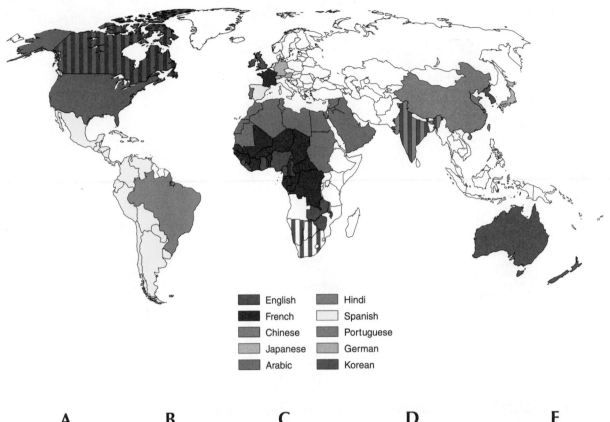

English	Hindi
French	Spanish
Chinese	Portuguese
Japanese	German
Arabic	Korean

A	B	C	D	E
100	**1000**	**10,000**	**100,000**	**1,000,000**

PRACTICE E

Part 1

1.	120	112	122
2.	1230	1240	1250
3.	4350	4360	4370
4.	10,490	10,480	10,411
5.	89,913	99,813	98,913

6.	100,611	100,601	100,661
7.	707,717	707,771	717,707
8.	515,850	515,580	505,515
9.	1,870,410	1,878,411	1,880,412
10.	20,550,312	12,550,320	21,555,312

Part 2

Japanese _____	Spanish _____
German _____	English _____
French _____	Chinese _____
Portuguese _____	Korean _____
Arabic _____	Hindi _____

Part 3

1.	186 million	106 million	6.	1.37 billion	1.37 million
2.	25 million	125 million	7.	322 million	310 million
3.	330 million	332 million	8.	17 million	72 million
4.	170 million	160 million	9.	75 million	64 million
5.	322 million	310 million	10.	33 million	330 million

UNIT 4   MONTHS AND DAYS

PRESENTATION A

PRACTICE A

Part 1

Part 2

A B C D E F G H J
K L M N O Q R S T
U V X Y Z

Part 3

	1.	2.	3.	4.	5.	6.	7.	8.	9.	10.
Yes										
No										

PRESENTATION B

1	2	3	4
JANUARY	FEBRUARY	MARCH	APRIL

5	6	7	8
MAY	JUNE	JULY	AUGUST

9	10	11	12
SEPTEMBER	OCTOBER	NOVEMBER	DECEMBER

PRACTICE B

Part 1

JANUARY

Sunday	Monday	Tuesday	Wednesday	Thursday	Friday	Saturday
			1	2	3	4
5	6	7	8	9	10	11
12	13	14	15	16	17	18
19	20	21	22	23	24	25
26	27	28	29	30	31	

FEBRUARY

Sunday	Monday	Tuesday	Wednesday	Thursday	Friday	Saturday
						1
2	3	4	5	6	7	8
9	10	11	12	13	14	15
16	17	18	19	20	21	22
23	24	25	26	27	28	

MARCH

Sunday	Monday	Tuesday	Wednesday	Thursday	Friday	Saturday
						1
2	3	4	5	6	7	8
9	10	11	12	13	14	15
16	17	18	19	20	21	22
23	24	25	26	27	28	29
30	31					

APRIL

Sunday	Monday	Tuesday	Wednesday	Thursday	Friday	Saturday
		1	2	3	4	5
6	7	8	9	10	11	12
13	14	15	16	17	18	19
20	21	22	23	24	25	26
27	28	29	30			

MAY

Sunday	Monday	Tuesday	Wednesday	Thursday	Friday	Saturday
				1	2	3
4	5	6	7	8	9	10
11	12	13	14	15	16	17
18	19	20	21	22	23	24
25	26	27	28	29	30	31

JUNE

Sunday	Monday	Tuesday	Wednesday	Thursday	Friday	Saturday
1	2	3	4	5	6	7
8	9	10	11	12	13	14
15	16	17	18	19	20	21
22	23	24	25	26	27	28
29	30					

JULY

Sunday	Monday	Tuesday	Wednesday	Thursday	Friday	Saturday
		1	2	3	4	5
6	7	8	9	10	11	12
13	14	15	16	17	18	19
20	21	22	23	24	25	26
27	28	29	30	31		

AUGUST

Sunday	Monday	Tuesday	Wednesday	Thursday	Friday	Saturday
					1	2
3	4	5	6	7	8	9
10	11	12	13	14	15	16
17	18	19	20	21	22	23
24	25	26	27	28	29	30
31						

SEPTEMBER

Sunday	Monday	Tuesday	Wednesday	Thursday	Friday	Saturday
	1	2	3	4	5	6
7	8	9	10	11	12	13
14	15	16	17	18	19	20
21	22	23	24	25	26	27
28	29	30				

OCTOBER

Sunday	Monday	Tuesday	Wednesday	Thursday	Friday	Saturday
		1	2	3	4	
5	6	7	8	9	10	11
12	13	14	15	16	17	18
19	20	21	22	23	24	25
26	27	28	29	30	31	

NOVEMBER

Sunday	Monday	Tuesday	Wednesday	Thursday	Friday	Saturday
						1
2	3	4	5	6	7	8
9	10	11	12	13	14	15
16	17	18	19	20	21	22
23	24	25	26	27	28	29
30						

DECEMBER

Sunday	Monday	Tuesday	Wednesday	Thursday	Friday	Saturday
	1	2	3	4	5	6
7	8	9	10	11	12	13
14	15	16	17	18	19	20
21	22	23	24	25	26	27
28	29	30	31			

Part 2

	1.	2.	3.	4.	5.	6.	7.	8.	9.	10.
Yes										
No										

READ & WRITE

Part 1

1. __ __ __

2. __ __ __ __

3. __ __ __ __

4. __ __ __ __ __

5. __ __ __ __ __

6. __ __ __ __ __ __

7. __ __ __ __ __ __ __ __ __

8. __ __ __ __ __ __ __ __ __

9. __ __ __ __ __ __ __ __

10. __ __ __ __ __ __ __

11. __ __ __ __ __ __ __ __

12. __ __ __ __ __ __ __

Part 2

1. _____ has two "R"s.

2. _____ has two "U"s.

3. _____ has two "A"s.

4. _____ has one "H."

5. _____ has two "O"s.

6. _____ has one "V."

7. _____ has one "P" and one "L."

8. _____ has one "U" and one "E."

9. _____ has one "L" and one "Y."

10. _____ and _____ have three "E"s.

JANUARY

Sunday	Monday	Tuesday	Wednesday	Thursday	Friday	Saturday
1	2	3	4	5	6	7
8	9	10	11	12	13	14
15	16	17	18	19	20	21
22	23	24	25	26	27	28
29	30	31				

PRACTICE C

JANUARY

Sunday	Monday	Tuesday	Wednesday	Thursday	Friday	Satur
1	2	3	4	5	6	7

READ & WRITE

Part 1

1. __ __ __ __ __ __

2. __ __ __ __ __ __

3. __ __ __ __ __ __

4. __ __ __ __ __ __ __

5. __ __ __ __ __ __ __ __

6. __ __ __ __ __ __ __ __

7. __ __ __ __ __ __ __ __ __

Part 2

1. Monday comes before _____.

2. Thursday comes before _____.

3. Tuesday comes before _____.

4. Saturday comes before _____.

5. Friday comes after _____.

6. Wednesday comes after _____.

7. Sunday comes after _____.

8. Thursday comes after _____.

9. Friday comes before _____.

10. Tuesday comes after _____.

11. Wednesday comes before _____.

12. Sunday comes before _____.

13. Saturday comes after _____.

14. Friday comes _____ Saturday.

15. Monday comes _____ Sunday.

16. Thursday comes _____ Wednesday.

17. Saturday comes _____ Sunday.

18. Wednesday comes _____ Tuesday.

Part 3

The French word for January Javier. The word for October Oktobre. The Spanish word April Abril. In Europe the of the months are almost the same. The name Park a Korean and it is also an name. Japanese words from Portuguese. Pan a Portuguese word but it is also a word.

I have a Spanish name.

You have a French name.

We have Korean names.

You have English names.

He has a German name.

They have Indian names.

She has a Portugese name.

UNIT 5   CALENDAR DATES AND SEASONS

PRESENTATION A

JANUARY						
Sunday	Monday	Tuesday	Wednesday	Thursday	Friday	Saturday
			1	2	3	4
5	6	7	8	9	10	11
12	13	14	15	16	17	18
19	20	21	22	23	24	25
26	27	28	29	30	31	

FEBRUARY						
Sunday	Monday	Tuesday	Wednesday	Thursday	Friday	Saturday
						1
2	3	4	5	6	7	8
9	10	11	12	13	14	15
16	17	18	19	20	21	22
23	24	25	26	27	28	

MARCH						
Sunday	Monday	Tuesday	Wednesday	Thursday	Friday	Saturday
						1
2	3	4	5	6	7	8
9	10	11	12	13	14	15
16	17	18	19	20	21	22
23	24	25	26	27	28	29
30	31					

APRIL						
Sunday	Monday	Tuesday	Wednesday	Thursday	Friday	Saturday
		1	2	3	4	5
6	7	8	9	10	11	12
13	14	15	16	17	18	19
20	21	22	23	24	25	26
27	28	29	30			

MAY						
Sunday	Monday	Tuesday	Wednesday	Thursday	Friday	Saturday
				1	2	3
4	5	6	7	8	9	10
11	12	13	14	15	16	17
18	19	20	21	22	23	24
25	26	27	28	29	30	31

JUNE						
Sunday	Monday	Tuesday	Wednesday	Thursday	Friday	Saturday
1	2	3	4	5	6	7
8	9	10	11	12	13	14
15	16	17	18	19	20	21
22	23	24	25	26	27	28
29	30					

JULY						
Sunday	Monday	Tuesday	Wednesday	Thursday	Friday	Saturday
		1	2	3	4	5
6	7	8	9	10	11	12
13	14	15	16	17	18	19
20	21	22	23	24	25	26
27	28	29	30	31		

AUGUST						
Sunday	Monday	Tuesday	Wednesday	Thursday	Friday	Saturday
					1	2
3	4	5	6	7	8	9
10	11	12	13	14	15	16
17	18	19	20	21	22	23
24	25	26	27	28	29	30
31						

SEPTEMBER						
Sunday	Monday	Tuesday	Wednesday	Thursday	Friday	Saturday
	1	2	3	4	5	6
7	8	9	10	11	12	13
14	15	16	17	18	19	20
21	22	23	24	25	26	27
28	29	30				

OCTOBER						
Sunday	Monday	Tuesday	Wednesday	Thursday	Friday	Saturday
			1	2	3	4
5	6	7	8	9	10	11
12	13	14	15	16	17	18
19	20	21	22	23	24	25
26	27	28	29	30	31	

NOVEMBER						
Sunday	Monday	Tuesday	Wednesday	Thursday	Friday	Saturday
						1
2	3	4	5	6	7	8
9	10	11	12	13	14	15
16	17	18	19	20	21	22
23	24	25	26	27	28	29
30						

DECEMBER						
Sunday	Monday	Tuesday	Wednesday	Thursday	Friday	Saturday
	1	2	3	4	5	6
7	8	9	10	11	12	13
14	15	16	17	18	19	20
21	22	23	24	25	26	27
28	29	30	31			

PRACTICE A

Part 1

	1.	2.	3.	4.	5.	6.	7.	8.	9.	10.
Yes										
No										

Part 2

1. January 5, 1993   January 6, 1993   January 7, 1993
2. February 4, 1998   February 5, 1998   February 6, 1998
3. March 7, 1999   March 8, 1999   March 9, 1999
4. April 10, 2010   April 11, 2010   April 12, 2010
5. May 1, 1949   May 2, 1949   May 3, 1949
6. June 1, 1997   June 11, 1997   June 12, 1997
7. July 2, 2013   July 3, 2013   July 13, 2013

8.	August 8, 1989	August 18, 1989	August 28, 1989
9.	September 14, 2005	September 4, 2005	September 24, 2005
10.	October 9, 1995	October 19, 1995	October 20, 1995
11.	November 20, 1994	November 30, 1994	November 12, 1994
12.	December 31, 1998	December 21, 1998	December 1, 1998

PRESENTATION B

1	2	3	4
1/2/99	2/2/99	3/2/99	4/2/99

5	6	7	8
5/2/99	6/2/99	7/2/99	8/2/99

9	10	11	12
9/2/99	10/2/99	11/2/99	12/2/99

PRACTICE B

Part 1

	A	B	C
1.	2/3/90	3/3/90	4/3/90
2.	10/10/97	11/10/97	9/10/97
3.	4/5/98	6/5/98	8/5/98
4.	8/18/12	9/18/12	10/18/12
5.	6/26/20	8/26/20	7/26/20
6.	1/20/99	2/20/99	3/20/99
7.	7/12/89	9/12/89	11/12/89
8.	5/30/03	6/30/03	4/30/03
9.	12/12/11	12/2/11	12/1/11
10.	3/31/09	3/30/09	3/3/09

READ & WRITE

Part 1

1. ___ / ___ / ___

2. ___ / ___ / ___

3. ___ / ___ / ___

4. ___ / ___ / ___

5. ___ / ___ / ___

6. ___ / ___ / ___

7. ___ / ___ / ___

8. ___ / ___ / ___

9. ___ / ___ / ___

10. ___ / ___ / ___

Part 2

1. 2/8/98 = _____

2. 6/14/99 = _____

3. 9/20/02 = _____

4. 5/30/96 = _____

5. 10/26/12 = _____

6. 4/12/96 = _____

7. 8/11/97 = _____

8. 1/5/98 = _____

9. 3/10/00 = _____

10. 12/12/04 = _____

Part 1

JANUARY

Sunday	Monday	Tuesday	Wednesday	Thursday	Friday	Saturday
			1	2	3	4
5	6	7	8	9	10	11
12	13	14	15	16	17	18
19	20	21	22	23	24	25
26	27	28	29	30	31	

FEBRUARY

Sunday	Monday	Tuesday	Wednesday	Thursday	Friday	Saturday
						1
2	3	4	5	6	7	8
9	10	11	12	13	14	15
16	17	18	19	20	21	22
23	24	25	26	27	28	

MARCH

Sunday	Monday	Tuesday	Wednesday	Thursday	Friday	Saturday
						1
2	3	4	5	6	7	8
9	10	11	12	13	14	15
16	17	18	19	20	21	22
23	24	25	26	27	28	29
30	31					

APRIL

Sunday	Monday	Tuesday	Wednesday	Thursday	Friday	Saturday
		1	2	3	4	5
6	7	8	9	10	11	12
13	14	15	16	17	18	19
20	21	22	23	24	25	26
27	28	29	30			

MAY

Sunday	Monday	Tuesday	Wednesday	Thursday	Friday	Saturday
				1	2	3
4	5	6	7	8	9	10
11	12	13	14	15	16	17
18	19	20	21	22	23	24
25	26	27	28	29	30	31

JUNE

Sunday	Monday	Tuesday	Wednesday	Thursday	Friday	Saturday
1	2	3	4	5	6	7
8	9	10	11	12	13	14
15	16	17	18	19	20	21
22	23	24	25	26	27	28
29	30					

JULY

Sunday	Monday	Tuesday	Wednesday	Thursday	Friday	Saturday
		1	2	3	4	5
6	7	8	9	10	11	12
13	14	15	16	17	18	19
20	21	22	23	24	25	26
27	28	29	30	31		

AUGUST

Sunday	Monday	Tuesday	Wednesday	Thursday	Friday	Saturday
					1	2
3	4	5	6	7	8	9
10	11	12	13	14	15	16
17	18	19	20	21	22	23
24	25	26	27	28	29	30
31						

SEPTEMBER

Sunday	Monday	Tuesday	Wednesday	Thursday	Friday	Saturday
	1	2	3	4	5	6
7	8	9	10	11	12	13
14	15	16	17	18	19	20
21	22	23	24	25	26	27
28	29	30				

OCTOBER

Sunday	Monday	Tuesday	Wednesday	Thursday	Friday	Saturday
		1	2	3	4	
5	6	7	8	9	10	11
12	13	14	15	16	17	18
19	20	21	22	23	24	25
26	27	28	29	30	31	

NOVEMBER

Sunday	Monday	Tuesday	Wednesday	Thursday	Friday	Saturday
						1
2	3	4	5	6	7	8
9	10	11	12	13	14	15
16	17	18	19	20	21	22
23	24	25	26	27	28	29
30						

DECEMBER

Sunday	Monday	Tuesday	Wednesday	Thursday	Friday	Saturday
	1	2	3	4	5	6
7	8	9	10	11	12	13
14	15	16	17	18	19	20
21	22	23	24	25	26	27
28	29	30	31			

Part 2

	1.	2.	3.	4.	5.	6.	7.
Yes							
No							

PRESENTATION D

Part 1

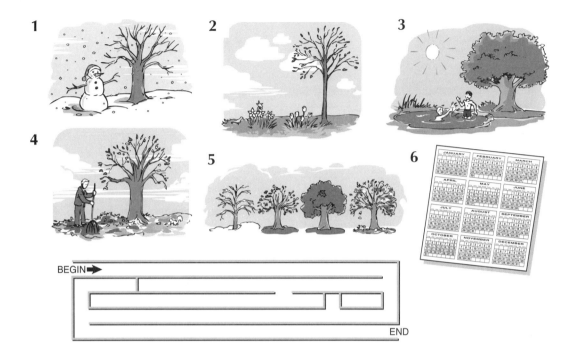

1

2

3

4

5

6

BEGIN ➡

END

Part 2

		JANUARY				
Sunday	Monday	Tuesday	Wednesday	Thursday	Friday	Saturday
			1	2	3	4
5	6	7	8	9	10	11
12	13	14	15	16	17	18
19	20	21	22	23	24	25
26	27	28	29	30	31	

		FEBRUARY				
Sunday	Monday	Tuesday	Wednesday	Thursday	Friday	Saturday
						1
2	3	4	5	6	7	8
9	10	11	12	13	14	15
16	17	18	19	20	21	22
23	24	25	26	27	28	

		MARCH				
Sunday	Monday	Tuesday	Wednesday	Thursday	Friday	Saturday
						1
2	3	4	5	6	7	8
9	10	11	12	13	14	15
16	17	18	19	20	(21)	22
23	24	25	26	27	28	29
30	31					

		APRIL				
Sunday	Monday	Tuesday	Wednesday	Thursday	Friday	Saturday
		1	2	3	4	5
6	7	8	9	10	11	12
13	14	15	16	17	18	19
20	21	22	23	24	25	26
27	28	29	30			

		MAY				
Sunday	Monday	Tuesday	Wednesday	Thursday	Friday	Saturday
				1	2	3
4	5	6	7	8	9	10
11	12	13	14	15	16	17
18	19	20	21	22	23	24
25	26	27	28	29	30	31

		JUNE				
Sunday	Monday	Tuesday	Wednesday	Thursday	Friday	Saturday
1	2	3	4	5	6	7
8	9	10	11	12	13	14
15	16	17	18	19	20	(21)
22	23	24	25	26	27	28
29	30					

		JULY				
Sunday	Monday	Tuesday	Wednesday	Thursday	Friday	Saturday
		1	2	3	4	5
6	7	8	9	10	11	12
13	14	15	16	17	18	19
20	21	22	23	24	25	26
27	28	29	30	31		

		AUGUST				
Sunday	Monday	Tuesday	Wednesday	Thursday	Friday	Saturday
					1	2
3	4	5	6	7	8	9
10	11	12	13	14	15	16
17	18	19	20	21	22	23
24	25	26	27	28	29	30
31						

		SEPTEMBER				
Sunday	Monday	Tuesday	Wednesday	Thursday	Friday	Saturday
	1	2	3	4	5	6
7	8	9	10	11	12	13
14	15	16	17	18	19	20
(21)	22	23	24	25	26	27
28	29	30				

		OCTOBER				
Sunday	Monday	Tuesday	Wednesday	Thursday	Friday	Saturday
			1	2	3	4
5	6	7	8	9	10	11
12	13	14	15	16	17	18
19	20	21	22	23	24	25
26	27	28	29	30	31	

		NOVEMBER				
Sunday	Monday	Tuesday	Wednesday	Thursday	Friday	Saturday
						1
2	3	4	5	6	7	8
9	10	11	12	13	14	15
16	17	18	19	20	21	22
23	24	25	26	27	28	29
30						

		DECEMBER				
Sunday	Monday	Tuesday	Wednesday	Thursday	Friday	Saturday
	1	2	3	4	5	6
7	8	9	10	11	12	13
14	15	16	17	18	19	20
(21)	22	23	24	25	26	27
28	29	30	31			

December 21 = December twenty-first = December 21

PRACTICE D

Part 1

	1.	2.	3.	4.	5.	6.	7.	8.	9.	10.
Yes										
No										

Part 2

1.	March 21	June 21	September 21
2.	March 20	September 20	June 20
3.	December 21	September 21	March 21
4.	September 20	June 20	December 20
5.	September 21	December 21	March 21
6.	June 20	September 20	December 20
7.	March 20	June 20	September 20
8.	December 21	March 21	June 21
9.	March 21	January 1	December 31
10.	September 21	December 31	December 21

READ & WRITE

Part 1

1. __ __ __ __ __ __
2. __ __ __ __ __ __
3. __ __ __
4. __ __ __ __
5. __ __ __ __ __ __
6. __ __ __ __ __
7. __ __ __ __ __ __
8. __ __ __ __ __ __ __

Part 2

1. _____ begins June 21.
2. _____ ends December 20.
3. _____ begins March 21.
4. _____ ends March 20.
5. _____ ends June 20.
6. _____ begins September 21.
7. Summer _____ September 20.
8. Winter _____ December 21.
9. The _____ begins January 1.
10. The year _____ December 31.

Part 3

There are months in a year. February 28 days. April, September, and November 30 days. January, March, July, August, and December have days. There are 365 in a year. The year January 1 and it December 31. There are seasons in a year. Spring March 21 and it June 20. When summer, autumn, and winter and end?

Winter is a season.   Summer and winter are seasons.

The first month is January.   The first two months are January and February.

February has 28 days.   July and August have 31 days.

REVIEW

Part 1

1. January _____ the first month of the year.

2. July and August _____ summer months.

3. February _____ 28 days.

4. December 31 _____ the last day of the year.

5. January and February _____ winter months.

6. April and September _____ 30 days.

7. November _____ the eleventh month of the year.

8. The summer months _____ June, July, and August.

9. A year _____ 12 months.

10. The last day of winter _____ March 20.

Part 2

1. _____ does winter begin?   _____

2. _____ season begins June 21?   _____

3. _____ day is the last day of the year? _____

4. _____ does spring end?   _____

5. _____ months have 30 days?   _____

6. _____ is the last month of the year? _____

7. _____ do summer and winter end?   _____

8. _____ does the year end?   _____

46

UNIT 6   OPPOSITES

PRESENTATION A

PRACTICE A

Part 1

	A	B	C
1.			
2.			
3.			
4.			
5.			

Part 2

	1.	2.	3.	4.	5.	6.	7.	8.	9.	10.
Yes										
No										

READ & WRITE

Part 1

1. ___ ___ ___
2. ___ ___ ___
3. ___ ___ ___
4. ___ ___ ___
5. ___ ___ ___
6. ___ ___ ___
7. ___ ___ ___
8. ___ ___ ___
9. ___ ___ ___ ___
10. ___ ___ ___ ___

11. ___ ___ ___ ___
12. ___ ___ ___
13. ___ ___ ___
14. ___ ___ ___
15. ___ ___ ___
16. ___ ___ ___ ___
17. ___ ___ ___ ___
18. ___ ___ ___ ___
19. ___ ___ ___ ___
20. ___ ___ ___ ___

Part 2

1. Day is the opposite of _____.

2. Hot is the opposite of _____.

3. _____ is the opposite of soft.

4. _____ is the opposite of dark.

5. Happy is the opposite of _____.

6. War is the opposite of _____.

7. _____ is the opposite of slow.

8. _____ is the opposite of male.

9. Little is the opposite of _____.

10. Dry is the opposite of _____.

PRACTICE B

Part 1

YES = TRUE		NO = FALSE

	1.	2.	3.	4.	5.	6.	7.	8.	9.	10.
True										
False										

Hot <u>isn't</u> the opposite of day. Hot <u>is</u> the opposite of cold.

Part 2

1. War (is / isn't) the opposite of peace.
2. Hot (is / isn't) the opposite of slow.
3. Begin (is / isn't) the opposite of happy.
4. War (is / isn't) the opposite of little.
5. Male (is / isn't) the opposite of female.
6. Big (is / isn't) the opposit of white.
7. Soft (is / isn't) the opposite of hard.
8. Summer (is / isn't) the opposite of winter.
9. Dry (is / isn't) the opposite of wet.
10. Night (is / isn't) the opposite of dark.

Part 3

Peace the opposite of war. War is and peace is. It true that is the opposite of happy? Hot is opposite of cold. Summer is and is cold. Is it true that is the of cold? Night is the of day. Night dark and day light. Is it that night the opposite light?

PRESENTATION C

50

Part 1

Part 2

	1.	2.	3.	4.	5.	6.	7.	8.	9.	10.
True										
False										

READ & WRITE

Part 1

1. __ __ __ __
2. __ __ __
3. __ __ __ __
4. __ __ __ __ __
5. __ __ __ __ __

6. __ __ __ __ __
7. __ __ __ __ __
8. __ __ __ __ __ __ __ __
9. __ __ __ __ __ __ __ __ __

Pillows <u>aren't</u> hard.   Pillows <u>are</u> soft.
Rocks <u>aren't</u> soft.   Rocks <u>are</u> hard.

Part 2

1. Girls (are / aren't) female.
2. Mice (are / aren't) big.
3. Rocks (are / aren't) soft.
4. Teeth (are / aren't) white.
5. Men (are / aren't) male.
6. Elephants (are / aren't) little.
7. Pillows (are / aren't) hard.
8. January and February (are / aren't) cold in Canada.
9. Mexico (and the United States are / aren't) in Europe.
10. July and August (are / aren't) summer months.

Part 3

In Canada, January and February cold. They are months. In Brazil, and February cold. They hot. When is winter in Canada, it summer Brazil. In Brazil seasons are the opposite the seasons Canada.

UNIT 7   NATURE

PRESENTATION A

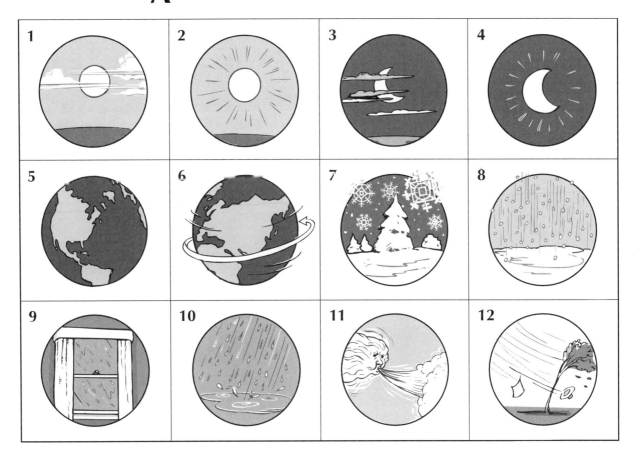

PRACTICE A

Part 1

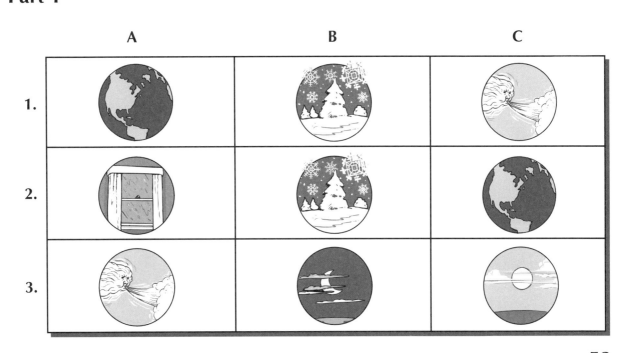

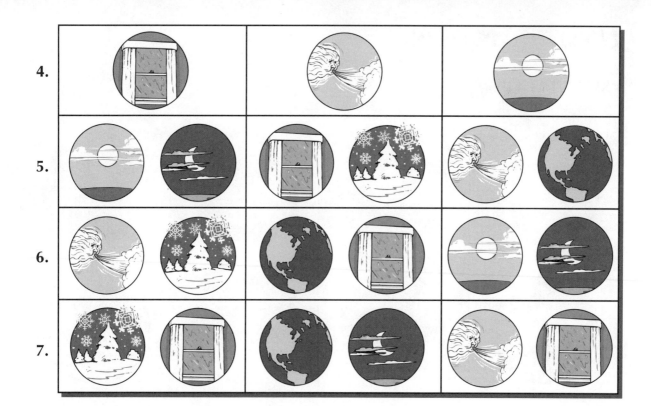

Part 2

	1.	2.	3.	4.	5.	6.	7.	8.	9.	10.
True										
False										

READ & WRITE

Part 1

1. __ __ __

2. __ __ __ __

3. __ __ __ __

4. __ __ __ __

5. __ __ __ __

6. __ __ __ __ __

7. __ __ __ __ __

8. __ __ __ __ __

9. __ __ __ __ __

10. __ __ __ __ __

The sun <u>shines</u> during the day. It <u>doesn't shine</u> at night.

Part 2

1. The sun | shines / doesn't shine | at night. It | shines / doesn't shine | during the day.

2. Rain | falls / doesn't fall | on the earth. It | falls / doesn't fall | on the moon.

3. Snow | falls / doesn't fall | in summer. It | falls / doesn't fall | in winter.

4. The moon | shines / doesn't shine | at night. It | shines / doesn't shine | during the day.

5. Snow | falls / doesn't fall | on the moon. It | falls / doesn't fall | on the earth.

6. The earth | turns / doesn't turn | all year.

7. The sun | shines / doesn't shine | in summer.

8. The wind | blows / doesn't blow | on the moon.

Part 3

Canada the are cold. Snow begins to fall October, and it end until May. The nights cold dark. In January February the doesn't after 6:00 P.M.

PRESENTATION B

PRACTICE B

Part 1

	A	B	C
1.			
2.			
3.			
4.			
5.			
6.			
7.			

Part 2

	1.	2.	3.	4.	5.	6.	7.	8.	9.	10.
Yes										
No										

READ & WRITE

Part 1

1. __ __ __ __

2. __ __ __ __

3. __ __ __ __ __

4. __ __ __ __ __

5. __ __ __ __ __

6. __ __ __ __ __ __

7. __ __ __ __ __ __ __

8. __ __ __ __ __ __ __

9. __ __ __ __ __ __

10. __ __ __ __ __ __ __

Birds <u>eat</u> insects. Sheep <u>don't eat</u> insects.

Part 2

1. Sheep
| eat |
| don't eat |
insects.

2. Cats
| eat |
| don't eat |
fish.

3. Sharks
| eat |
| don't eat |
flowers.

4. Birds
| eat |
| don't eat |
insects.

5. People
| eat |
| don't eat |
spiders.

6. Sheep
| eat |
| don't eat |
flowers.

7. Cats
| eat |
| don't eat |
flies.

8. People
| eat |
| don't eat |
rocks.

9. Elephants
| eat |
| don't eat |
fish.

10. Insects
| eat |
| don't eat |
flowers.

Elephants <u>don't eat</u> birds, but cats <u>do eat</u> birds. = Elephants <u>don't eat</u> birds, but cats <u>do</u>.
Sheep <u>eat</u> flowers, but people <u>don't eat</u> flowers. = Sheep <u>eat</u> flowers, but people <u>don't</u>.

Part 3

1. Elephants | eat / don't eat | birds, but cats | do / don't | .

2. Spiders | eat / don't eat | flowers, but sheep | do / don't | .

3. Cats | eat / don't eat | fish, but elephants | do / don't | .

4. Sheep | eat / don't eat | insects, but birds | do / don't | .

5. Sharks | eat / don't eat | fish, but spiders | do / don't | .

6. Cats | eat / don't eat | birds, but elephants | do / don't | .

7. Sharks | eat / don't eat | flies, but spiders | do / don't | .

8. Sheep | eat / don't eat | flowers, but cats | do / don't | .

9. People | eat / don't eat | fish, but sheep | do / don't | .

> The sun <u>shines</u> in summer.   <u>Does</u> the sun <u>shine</u> in summer?
> Sharks <u>eat</u> fish.   <u>Do</u> sharks <u>eat</u> fish?

Part 4

Examples: <u>Does</u> the sun shine in summer? Yes it <u>shines</u> in summer.

<u>Do</u> sharks eat fish? Yes, they <u>eat</u> fish.

1.   _____ the moon shine at night? Yes, it _____ at night.

2.   _____ spiders eat flies? Yes, they _____ flies.

3.   _____ snow fall in winter? Yes, it _____ in winter.

4.   _____ cats eat birds? Yes, they _____ birds.

5.   _____ people eat fish? Yes, they _____ fish.

6.   _____ the earth turn all year? Yes, it _____ all year.

7.   _____ sharks eat flowers? No, they _____ _____ flowers.

8.   _____ the snow fall in summer? No, it _____ _____ in summer.

9.   _____ spiders and birds eat insects? Yes, they _____ insects.

10.   _____ the snow and the rain fall on the moon?

   No, they _____ _____ on the moon.

UNIT 8   GOING PLACES

PRESENTATION A

PRACTICE A

Part 1

	1.	2.	3.	4.	5.	6.	7.	8.	9.	10.
Yes										
No										

Part 2

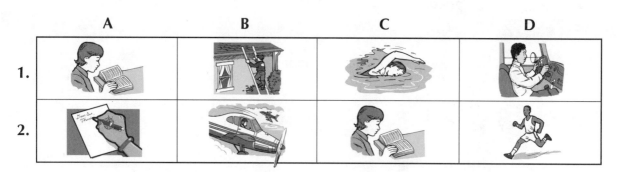

Part 3

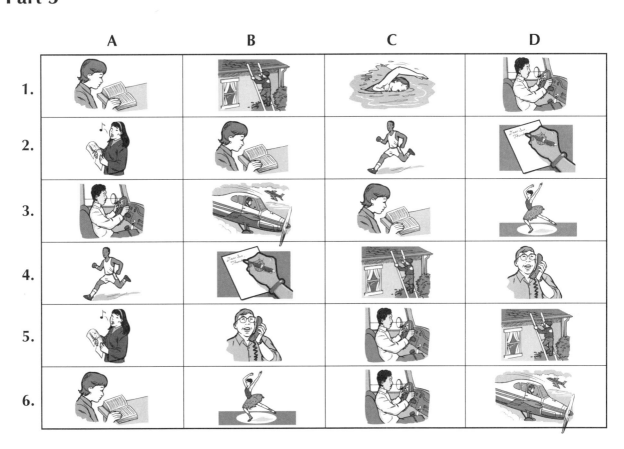

READ & WRITE

Part 1

1. __ __ __

2. __ __ __

3. __ __ __ __

4. __ __ __ __

5. __ __ __ __

6. __ __ __ __

7. __ __ __ __ __

8. __ __ __ __ __

9. __ __ __ __ __

Fish <u>can</u> swim.   Sheep <u>cannot</u> fly. = Sheep <u>can't</u> fly.

Part 2

Example: fish / swim / they / run
<u>Fish</u> can <u>swim</u>, but <u>they</u> can't <u>run</u>.

1. elephants / run / they / climb

   _____

2. birds / sing / they / dance

   _____

3. cats / fly / they / run

   _____

4. sharks / run / they / swim

   _____

5. spiders / climb / they / fly

   _____

PRESENTATION B

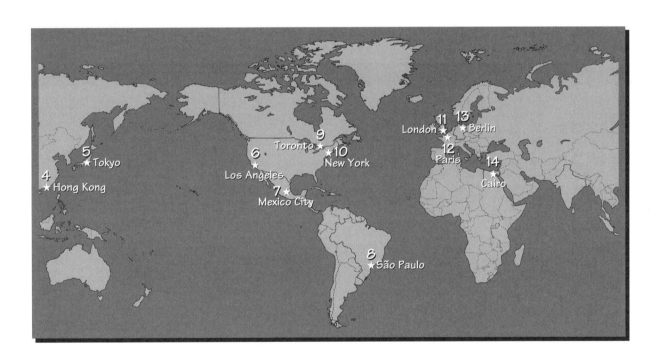

PRACTICE B

	1.	2.	3.	4.	5.	6.	7.	8.	9.	10.
Yes										
No										

PRACTICE C

1.	10 hrs., 30 min.	14 hrs., 30 min.	24 hrs., 15 min.
2.	6 hrs., 30 min.	3 hrs., 40 min.	4 hrs., 30 min.
3.	15 hrs., 30 min.	5 hrs., 15 min.	11 hrs., 30 min.
4.	20 hrs.	12 hrs.	3 hrs.
5.	10 days, 12 hrs.	5 days, 12 hrs.	3 days, 12 hrs.
6.	10 hrs., 15 min.	3 hrs., 15 min.	15 hrs., 10 min.
7.	7 hrs., 45 min.	6 hrs., 45 min.	16 hrs., 45 min.
8.	13 hrs.	3 hrs.	30 hrs.
9.	11 hrs., 55 min.	11 hrs., 35 min.	11 hrs., 25 min.
10.	5 hrs., 8 min.	8 hrs., 5 min.	8 hrs., 15 min.

READ & WRITE

Part 1

1. __ __ __

2. __ __ __ __ __

3. __ __ __ __ __

4. __ __ __ __ __

5. __ __ __ __ __ __

6. __ __ __ __ __

7. __ __ __ __ __ __ __

8. __ __ __ __ __

9. __ __ __ __ __ __ __

10. __ __ __ __ __ __ __ __

11. __ __ __ __ __ __

12. __ __ __ __ __ __ __ __

13. __ __ __ __ __ __
    __ __ __ __

14. __ __ __
    __ __ __ __ __ __ __

Part 2

Examples: New York / Toronto / bus
People <u>can go</u> from <u>New York</u> to <u>Toronto</u> by <u>bus</u>.

New York / Tokyo / bus
People <u>can't go</u> from <u>New York</u> to <u>Tokyo</u> by <u>bus</u>.

1. Paris / Los Angeles / train

_____

2. Hong Kong / New York / plane

_____

3. Mexico City / Los Angeles / bus

_____

4. Berlin / Paris / train

_____

5. Cairo / London / bus

_____

6. Tokyo / Toronto / plane

_____

7. Los Angeles / New York / train

_____

8. São Paulo / Berlin / bus

_____

9. Hong Kong / Tokyo / plane

_____

Part 3

Summer is a season to get Los Angeles New York by bus. It takes days, but you talk to people read. The sun all day, but it hot in the . In winter when the is falling, it take four or five to go from Los Angeles New York. I don't by bus winter. I by plane. It only hours.

UNIT 9   HERE AND THERE

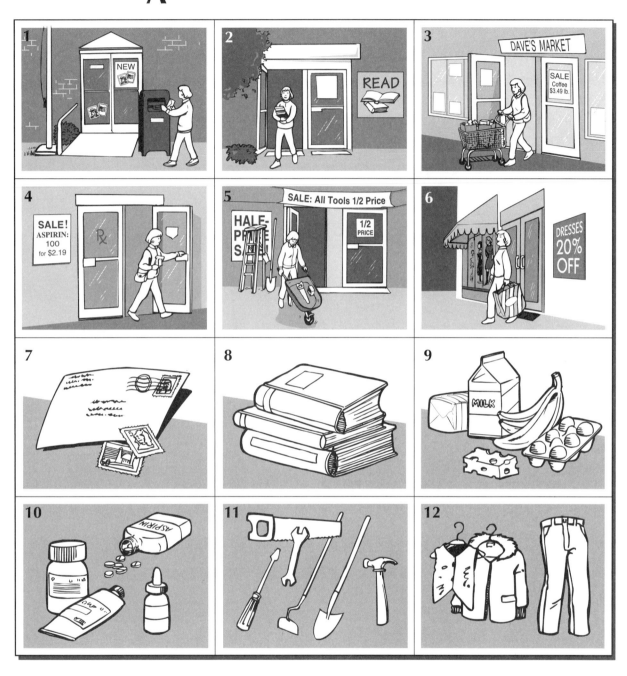

PRACTICE A

	1.	2.	3.	4.	5.	6.	7.	8.	9.	10.
Yes										
No										

READ & WRITE

Part 1

1. __ __ __ __ store

2. __ __ __ __ __ __ __ __ store

3. __ __ __ __ __ __ __ __ __ __ store

4. __ __ __ __   __ __ __ __ __ __

5. __ __ __ __ __ __

6. __ __ __ __ __ __ __ __ __ __ __

7. __ __ __ __

8. __ __ __ __ __ __

9. __ __ __ __ __

10. __ __ __ __ __

11. __ __ __ __ __ __ __

12. __ __ __ __ __ __ __ __

Part 2

Examples: People ⟮get⟯ / don't get stamps at a post office.

People get / ⟮don't get⟯ stamps at a library.

1. People ⎡ get / don't get ⎤ medicine at a hardware store.

2. People ⎡ get / don't get ⎤ clothes at a department store.

3. People ⎡ get / don't get ⎤ food at a library.

4. People ⎡ get / don't get ⎤ tools at a hardware store.

5. People ⎡ get / don't get ⎤ books at a post office.

6. People ⎡ get / don't get ⎤ food at a supermarket.

7. People ⎡ get / don't get ⎤ medicine at a drug store.

8. People ⎡ get / don't get ⎤ tools at a library.

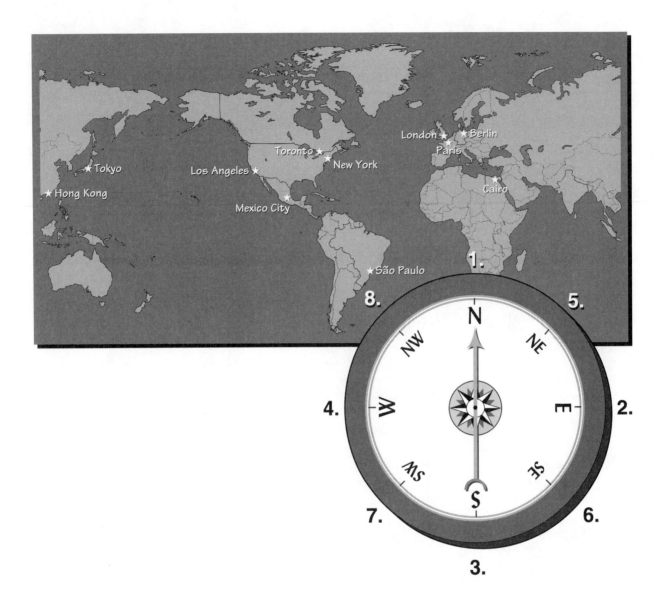

	1.	2.	3.	4.	5.	6.	7.	8.	9.	10.
Yes										
No										

READ & WRITE

Part 1

1. __ __ __ __ __

2. __ __ __ __

3. __ __ __ __

4. __ __ __ __ __

5. __ __ __ __ __ __ __ __ __

6. __ __ __ __ __ __ __ __ __

7. __ __ __ __ __ __ __ __ __

8. __ __ __ __ __ __ __ __

Part 2

1.	northwest	southwest	southeast
2.	southeast	southwest	northwest
3.	northeast	northwest	southwest
4.	southeast	southwest	northeast
5.	northeast	northwest	southwest
6.	southwest	southeast	northeast
7.	northwest	northeast	southwest
8.	northeast	northwest	southeast
9.	northwest	northeast	southwest
10.	southwest	northwest	northeast

Part 3

In when the snow begins to, the birds Canada and the United States fly to Mexico. In Mexico it cold, and the birds get food. Sun shines winter. In spring the begins to fall the United States and Canada. The earth green, and the birds fly to the flowers and of spring.

Part 4

Part 5

	1.	2.	3.	4.	5.	6.	7.	8.	9.	10.
Yes										
No										

74

UNIT 10   CATEGORIES

PRESENTATION A

1

red   white

blue

green   orange

2

1   50   6   10

100   2,000

3

A   R   F   Z

P   N   X   Y

4

January 4, 1971   July 4, 1776

9/20/44   10/22/73

May 9, 1991   Augut 2, 1906

5

Tuesday   Sunday

Friday   Thursday

Monday

6

June   October   April

August   July

May

7

spring

autumn

summer

8

London   New York

Paris

Tokyo   Cairo

9

Canada   Japan

Brazil   Mexico

10

Asia

North America

South America   Africa

11

German   Spanish

Korean   English

Japanese

12

east

south

north

PRACTICE A

Part 1

	1.	2.	3.	4.	5.	6.	7.	8.	9.	10.
Yes										
No										

	11.	12.	13.	14.	15.	16.	17.	18.	19.	20.
Yes										
No										

Part 2

1.	June	west	green
2.	9, 11, 12	M, N, O	10/26/40
3.	São Paulo	Canada	Asia
4.	10, 20, 30	X, Y, Z	May
5.	Germany	Korea	Europe
6.	Japan	India	Chinese
7.	winter & spring	north & south	gray & orange
8.	November 23, 1969	$84.95	12:30
9.	July & August	summer & autumn	Wednesday & Thursday
10.	March & April	spring & summer	east & west
11.	brown	south	Cairo
12.	Sunday	February	autumn

READ & WRITE

Part 1

1. __ __ __ __

2. __ __ __ __ __ __

3. __ __ __ __ __

4. __ __ __ __ __ __ __

5. __ __ __ __ __ __

6. __ __ __ __ __ __

7. __ __ __ __ __ __ __

8. __ __ __ __ __ __ __ __ __

9. __ __ __ __ __ __ __

10. __ __ __ __ __ __ __ __ __

11. __ __ __ __ __ __ __ __ __

12. __ __ __ __ __ __ __ __ __ __

Part 2

| is/isn't | are/aren't |

1. Canada _____ a city, but it _____ a country.

2. X, Y, Z _____ numbers, but they _____ letters.

3. Wednesday and Thursday _____ days, but they _____ months.

4. Green _____ a month, but it _____ a color.

5. Asia _____ a country, but it _____ a continent.

6. 10 and 100 _____ numbers, but they _____ letters.

7. North and south _____ dates, but they _____ directions.

8. January 4th _____ a date, but it _____ a color.

9. May _____ a season, but it _____ a month.

10. Spanish and Japanese _____ countries, but they _____ languages.

PRACTICE B

Part 1

1. to get clothes   to get tools   to get books

2. to get stamps   to get clothes   to get medicine

3. to get medicine   to get tools   to get books

4. to get stamps   to get clothes   to get medicine

5. to get clothes   to get books   to get tools

Part 2

Examples: *What* do we get at the library?   books
          Why do we go to the library?   to get books
          Where do we get books?   at the library

1. _____ do we get at the drugstore?   medicine

2. _____ do we get stamps?   at the post office

3. _____ do we go to the supermarket?   to get food

4. _____ do we get tools?   at the hardware store

5. _____ do we go to the post office?   to get stamps

6. _____ do we get at the department store?   clothes

7. _____ do we go to the library?   to get books

8. _____ do we get medicine?   at the drugstore

REVIEW TESTS

REVIEW TEST: Units 1 & 2

Part A

1. _____   1. _____   1. _____

2. _____   2. _____   2. _____

3. _____   3. _____   3. _____

4. _____   4. _____   4. _____

5. _____   5. _____   5. _____

Part B

Example: one twenty = 1:20

1. four ten =   5. three fifty - six =

2. six twenty - five =   6. eight fourteen =

3. eleven thirty =   7. two thirty - five =

4. twelve forty - five =   8. seven fifty - nine =

Part C

Example: red
                                          pink
                   white

1. _____
                                        orange
2. _____

3. _____
                                         gray
4. _____

5. _____
                                         green
6. _____

7. _____
                                          tan
8. _____

9. _____
                                        purple
10. _____

Part D

is	are	am

Examples: The boy _____is_____ wearing red.

The cars _____are_____ red.

1. The American flag _____ red, white, and blue.

2. The Canadian flag and the Japanese flag _____ red and white.

3. The Mexican flag _____ green, orange, and white.

4. I _____ wearing white.

5. You _____ wearing blue.

6. They _____ in the black car.

Part E

Example: D A C A N A I N = C A N A D I A N

1. N K O E R A = _____

2. N D N I A I = _____

3. T N E G P Y A I = _____

4. M N A C I A R E = _____

5. Z N I L I R B A A = _____

REVIEW TEST: Units 1 - 4

Part A

Example: _____20_____ + _____30_____ = 50

1. _____ + _____ = 80

2. _____ − _____ = 60

3. _____ + _____ = 90

4. _____ − _____ = 75

5. _____ + _____ = 130

6. _____ − _____ = 160

7. _____ − _____ = 600

8. _____ + _____ = 1,250

9. _____ + _____ = 1,020

10. _____ − _____ = 5,000

Part B

Example:  $13.04

1.

2.

3.

4.

5.

Part C

is	are

Example: Canada _____is_____ in North America.

1. Egypt _____ in Africa.

2. China and India _____ in Asia.

3. Mexico and the United States _____ in North America.

4. Brazil _____ in South America.

5. France and Germany _____ in Europe.

Part D

Arabic	English	French	German	Hindi	Potuguese	Spanish

Example: In the United States they speak _____English_____.

1. In Mexico they speak _____.

2. In Egypt they speak _____.

3. In India they speak _____.

4. In Brazil they speak _____.

5. In Canada they speak _____ and _____.

Part E

has	have

Example: I _____have_____ a Japanese flag.

1. We _____ a Mexican flag.

2. Canada _____ six letters: C, N, and D plus three A's.

3. September and April _____ 30 days.

4. China _____ 1,000,000,000 people.

Part F

is underlined	is circled
are underlined	are circled

ⒻEⒷRUAⓇY AⓊGUⓈⓉ DEⒸEMⒷER

Example: The F in February ____is circled____.

1. The Y in February _____.

2. The two U's in August _____.

3. The two R's in February _____.

4. The B in December _____.

5. The three E's in December _____.

Part G

after	before

Example: Monday comes ____before____ Tuesday.

1. Saturday comes _____ Friday.

2. June comes _____ July.

3. February comes _____ January.

4. Y comes _____ Z.

5. 100 comes _____ 99.

6. Sunday comes _____ Monday.

7. April comes _____ March.

8. 2000 comes _____ 1999.

9. United comes _____ States.

10. O P comes _____ M N.

Part H

1.	before **B**	speak English
2.	pink	China
3.	in Africa	DAY
4.	blue, white, and red	red and white
5.	322,000,000 people	T H U R D A Y
6.	red circle	Japanese flag
7.	in Asia	**A**
8.	after MON	Egypt
9.	**S** is missing.	French flag
10.	three **E's**	July
11.	before August	December

REVIEW TEST: Units 1 – 6

Part A

December	elephants	Friday	mice	night	October
pillows	rocks	slow	summer	teeth	winter

Examples: (What are soft?) _____ pillows _____

(What aren't soft?) _____ rocks _____

1. _____

2. _____

3. _____

4. _____

5. _____

6. _____

7. _____

8. _____

9. _____

10. _____

Part B

Example: (The opposite of black is _____.)   green   (white)   red

1. Sunday   Tuesday   Saturday

2. March   April   May

3. Friday   Sunday   Monday

4.	November	December	January
5.	28	30	31
6.	30	365	100
7.	May	February	July
8.	boy	man	girl
9.	Spanish	Portuguese	French
10.	January	February	March

Part C

begins	ends

Example: Winter _____begins_____ December 21st.

1. Summer _____ June 21st.

2. Winter _____ March 20th.

3. Spring _____ June 20th.

4. The year _____ on December 31st.

5. The year _____ on January 1st.

6. February _____ on the 28th.

7. *Japan* _____ with *J* and _____ with *N*.

8. The week _____ on Sunday and _____ on Saturday.

Part D

Example: A J U N Y R A = J A N U A R Y

1. L R P I A = _____

2. B P S T E E M R E = _____

3. G T U S A U = _____

4. R R F U E Y A B = _____

5. M N B O R V E E = _____

Part E

Example: Fifty _____plus_____ fifty is 100.
        (plus / minus)

1. The people in the United States speak _____.
                                        (German / English)

2. The French flag is blue, white, and _____.
                                        (yellow / red)

3. China is in _____.
(Asia / Europe)

4. Ninety _____ sixty is 30.
(plus / minus)

5. Day is the opposite of _____.
(light / night)

6. June is the _____ month of the year.
(fifth / sixth)

7. Brazil _____ in North America.
(is / isn't)

8. The Japanese flag and the Canadian flag _____ red and white.
(are / aren't)

9. The Egyptians speak _____.
(Hindi / Arabic)

10. January is the _____ month of the year.
(first / last)

11. August comes _____ July.
(before / after)

12. Nights are _____.
   (light / dark)

13. In _____ the people speak English and French.
   (Mexico / Canada)

14. Forty-nine comes _____ fifty.
   (before / after)

15. 1,037,000,000 people speak _____.
   (English / Chinese)

REVIEW TEST: Units 1 – 8

Part A

Example: (What can swim?)   (fish)   spiders   flowers

1. sheep   spiders   birds

2. cats   sharks   the wind

3. the earth   elephants   fish

4. the wind   the moon   the sun

5. the wind   flowers   the sun

6. the earth   rain   the moon

7. sharks   flowers   spiders

8. sheep   cats   sharks

9. the moon   birds   flowers

10. Chinese   Japanese   Spanish

Part B

Africa	Asia	Brazil	Canada
England	France	Germany	Japan
	North America	the United States	

Example: (Where is New York?) in ____the United States____

1. in _____   3. in _____

2. in _____   4. in _____

5. in _____   8. in _____

6. in _____   9. in _____

7. in _____   10. in _____

Part C

| is | isn't | are | aren't | can | can't |

Examples: Birds _____*can*_____ fly.   Snow _____*is*_____ white.

Summer _____*isn't*_____ cold.

1. Rain _____ dry.

2. Elephants _____ fly.

3. People _____ talk.

4. Pillows _____ soft.

5. The moon _____ pink.

6. Mice _____ big.

7. The moon _____ wet.

102

8. X, Y, and Z _____ last.

9. The sun _____ hot.

10. The earth _____ circle the sun.

Part D

1. hot   elephants

2. cold   flowers

3. dry   the moon

4. wet   night

5. dark   rain

6. hard   rocks

7. gray   sharks

8. 12 months   snow

9. big fish   the sun

10. red, white, pink, yellow, blue   one year

Part E

Do	Does

Example: _____Does_____ snow fall in winter?

1. _____ the sun shine?

2. _____ spiders eat flies?

3. _____ birds sing?

4. _____ people read and write?

5. _____ the wind blow?

Part F

do	don't	does	doesn't

Example: Spiders _____don't_____ swim, but fish _____do_____.

1. Elephants _____ climb, but cats _____.

2. Birds _____ read, but people _____.

3. The wind _____ shine, but the sun _____.

4. Sharks _____ eat flowers, but sheep _____.

5. The sun _____ circle the earth, but the moon _____.

104

REVIEW TEST: Units 1 – 10

Part A

	Yes	No
1.		
2.		
3.		
4.		
5.		
6.		
7.		
8.		
9.		
10.		
11.		
12.		
13.		
14.		
15.		
16.		
17.		
18.		
19.		
20.		
21.		
22.		
23.		
24.		
25.		

Part B

Example: (What has twenty-eight days?)   (February)   April   July

1. green   red   white

2. summer   winter   spring

3. March 21   June 21   September 21

4. Portuguese   Japanese   Spanish

5. sharks   fish   spiders

6. in summer   in autumn   in winter

7. June 20   September 20   December 20

8. at night   in the day   in the sun

9. one season   six seasons   one year

10. the earth   the moon   the year

Part C

is/isn't	are/aren't	do/don't	does/doesn't

1. Elephants _____ climb, but they _____ run.

2. January _____ a month, but it _____ a season.

3. Rain _____ fall on the moon, but it _____ fall

   on the earth.

4. The people in Brazil _____ speak Spanish, but they

   _____ speak Portuguese.

5. **S** _____ a letter, but it _____ a number.

6. Birds _____ eat rocks, but they _____ eat insects.

7. People _____ get medicine at a library, but they _____

   get it at a drugstore.

8. Pink and orange _____ colors, but they _____ directions.

9. The sun _____ shine at night, but it _____ shine in

   the day.

10. The Canadian and Japanese flags _____ red and white, but they

    _____ red, white, and blue.

Part D

April	Canada	Japanese	Portuguese	summer
Arabic	Egypt	July	São Paulo	Thursday
Asia	English	Korea	September	Tokyo
autumn	green	Los Angeles	south	Toronto
Brazil	January	10/26/40	spring	winter

CITIES

_____

_____

_____

_____

COUNTRIES

_____

_____

_____

_____

LANGUAGES

_____

_____

_____

MONTHS

_____

_____

_____

SEASONS

_____

_____